A is for Ape

by Dana E. McKee

A is for Ape
Fourth Edition
Copyright circa 2010

Create Space Published A is for Ape by Dana E. McKee, March 2010
Updated April 2014

ISBN 978-0615569420

All rights reserved. No part of this book may be reproduced, stored, or transmitted in any form or by any means—electronic, mechanical, photocopy, recording, scanning, or other—except for brief quotations in reviews or articles, without prior written permission from the author.

Scripture quotes are from various versions of the Bible. They are:

The Holy Bible, New International Version, NIV Copyright 1973, 1978, 1984, 2010 by Biblica, Inc., used by permission. All rights reserved worldwide.

Scripture taken from the NEW AMERICAN STANDARD BIBLE Copyright 1960, 1962, 1963, 1968, 1971, 1973, 1975, 1977, 1995 by The Lockman Foundation. Used by permission.

Scripture taken from the New King James Version (NKJV) Copyright circa 1982 by Thomas Nelson, Inc. Used by permission. All rights reserved.

Scripture quotations marked HCSB are taken from the Holman Christian Standard Bible. Copyright 1999, 2000, 2002, 2003 by Holman Bible Publishers. Used by permission. Holman Christian Standard Bible, Holman CSB, and HCSB are Federally registered trademarks of Holman Bible Publishers.

This book is dedicated to all our grandchildren.
So far that includes: Jolyn, Sam, Seth, Oren, Bria, Ariel, Zion, Kailyn, Nevaeh, and Sophie.

God made us. He set down an account of creation and gave it to Adam and Eve. They preserved it, wrote down their own story (which follows God's in the beginning of the Book of Genesis) and made sure these histories, along with other historical accounts, poems and songs, prophecies, etc., were carefully guarded through many years. Noah's family got the first of these important works safely through the Flood. Succeeding generations passed them down to Moses, who wrote them in the form we treasure today.

Believe God. Believe Adam and Eve, my children. Distrust Darwin and others who suppose and guess at all kinds of "might have been's and possibly's."

Much can be known about God by looking carefully at His world, His moon, His planets, stars and galaxies, the amazing plant and animal life all around, and us, ourselves. But more can be known through the written revelation of Himself. Do not let doubters and scoffers turn you from that good Book. In it is life; in it is nourishment and refreshment for your soul. Drink from its fountain. Take your own doubts to the pages of the Bible, God's Book. Study it. Scrutinize it, even. It can stand up.

I hope this little book will help you to teach letters and sounds to your children. But more than that, may you glimpse here that God's Word is fun and true. All of it. Even Genesis.

A is for Ape

With peoply shape.
Though it fit God's plans
To give the ape hands,
His folks and your mother's
Aren't cousins or brothers.

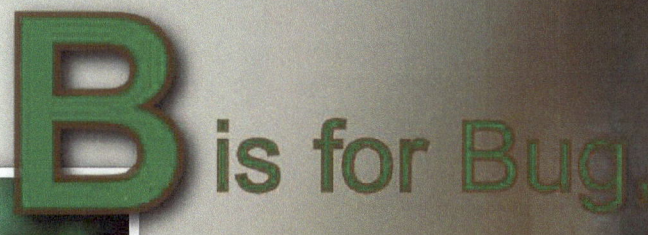

B is for Bug,

a six-legged wonder,
and hopper and buzzer
and borer and walker.

(Suppose Mrs. Noah
had brought her
fly-swatter!...)

*God created bugs,
and He created apes.
He made huge stars
And tiny snowflakes.*

*God made the turtle
and things that are purple!*

C means Creation.
God called His world good.

D is for Daytime.
God's sun lights the wood.

E is for Evening.

By the sixth one,
Creation complete, God was all done.
The seventh, He rested, earth's week-rythm blessed.
Though God was not tired, He graced us with rest.

G is for God.
Father, Spirit, Son -
Three distinct yet One.

*God is awesome;
He can save us!*

J is for Jubal,

*Who made flutes and lyres.
Listed among the grandkids of Cain,
Jubal's a real guy - not myth -
that is plain.*

L is for Lamech

Whose famous son, Noah,
The zoo-keeper/ builder
Was also a preacher.

"Judgment approaches!...
Come, help build the boat.
Soon it will house us
And insects
And goats...
The Flood sure
   will drown things,
But this Ark will
   float!"

M is for Monarchs

Who fluttered and flitted;
Clover they visited...
Then wafted and drifted
Until they were lifted
Into Noah's Ark,
A safe place to park.

N is for Noah.

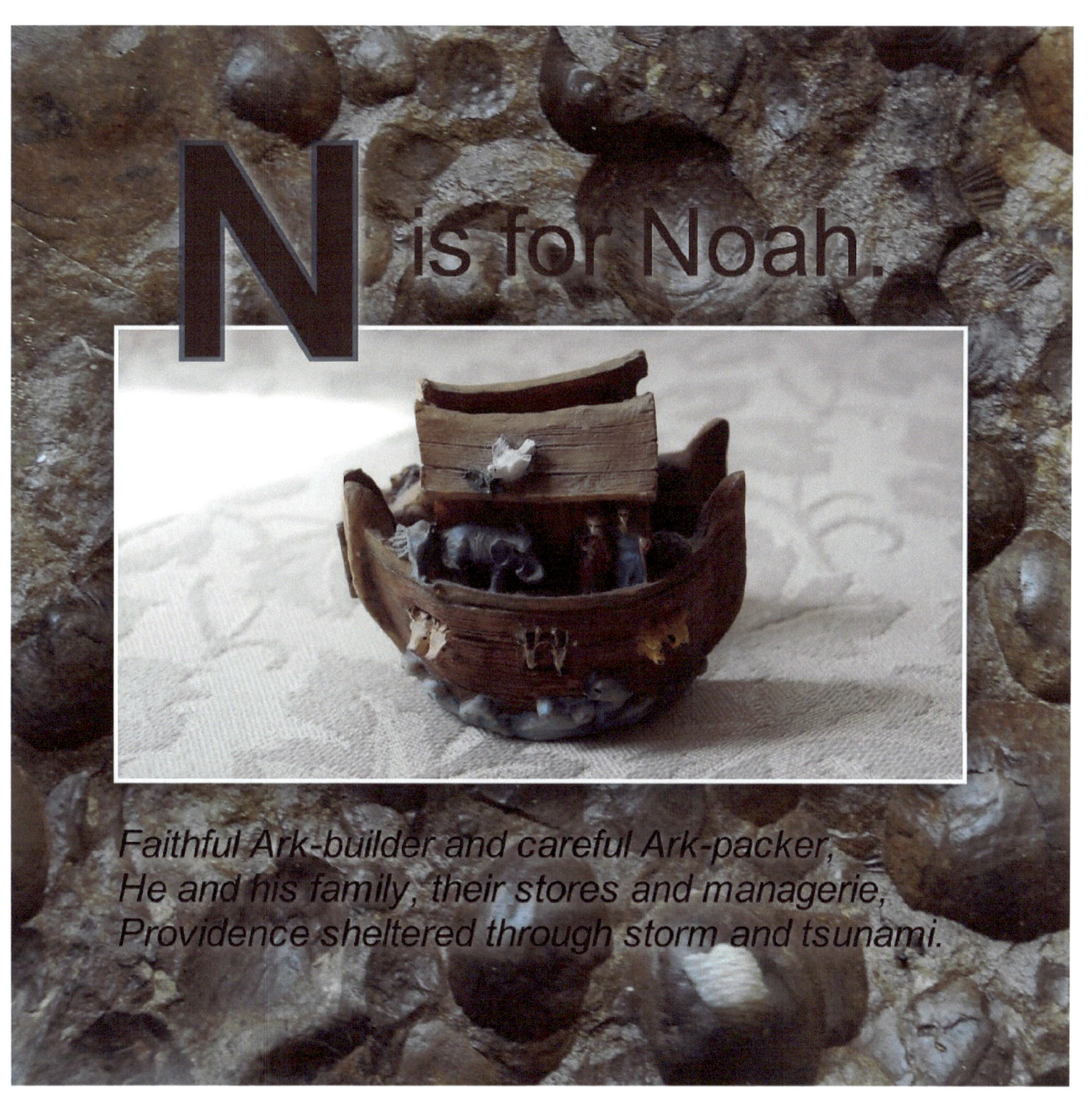

Faithful Ark-builder and careful Ark-packer,
He and his family, their stores and managerie,
Providence sheltered through storm and tsunami.

O is for Oats...

*Food for people and blue jays
Hamsters and goats
(and horses!)*

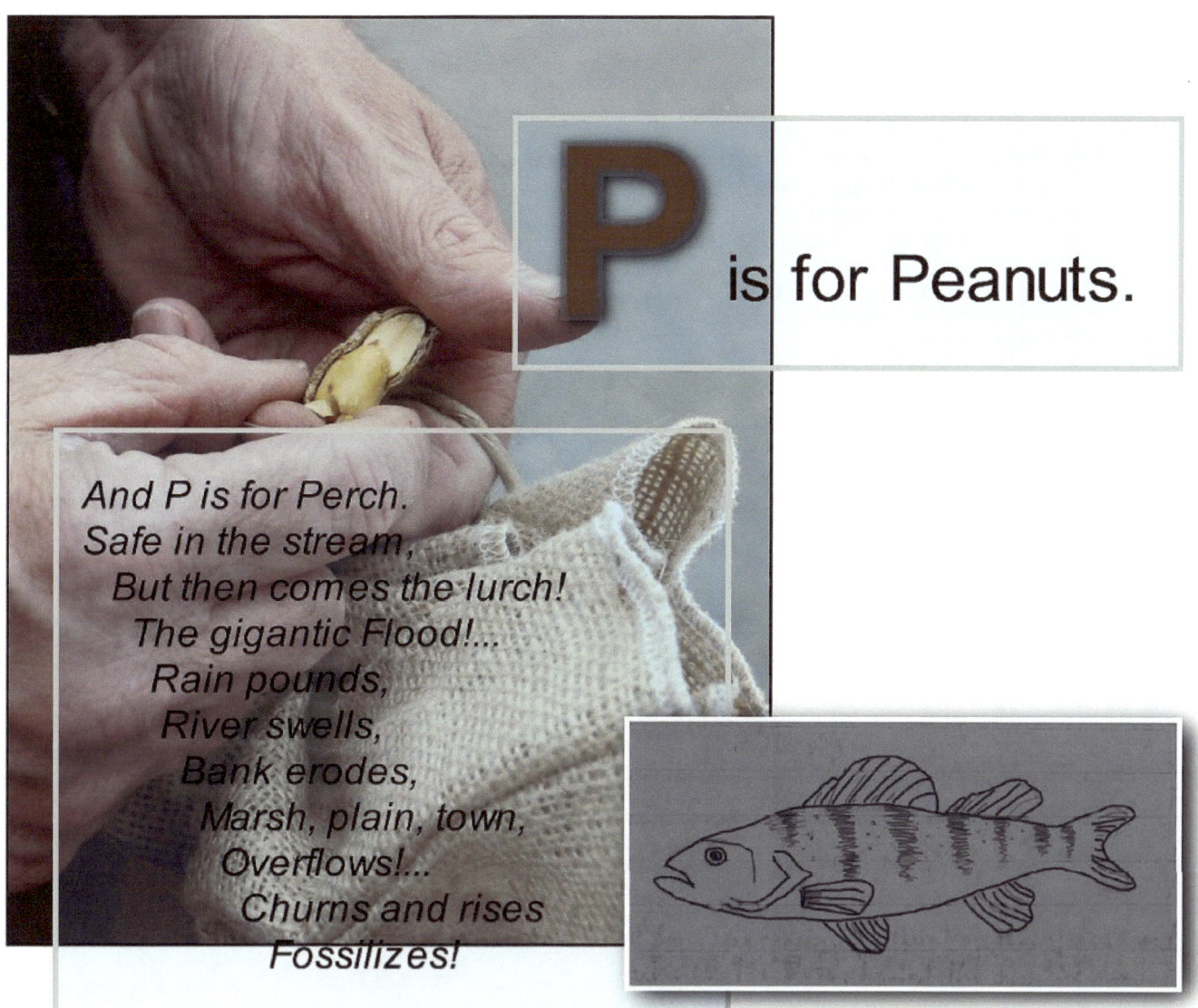

P is for Peanuts.

And P is for Perch.
Safe in the stream,
 But then comes the lurch!
  The gigantic Flood!...
   Rain pounds,
    River swells,
     Bank erodes,
      Marsh, plain, town,
       Overflows!...
        Churns and rises
         Fossilizes!

Or, twisting, tumbling
The perch is free
In the sea!

Q is for Quarreling,

*Quaking,
Shaking!...
Lava spilling,
Thunder roaring!
Canyons splitting,
Mountains soaring!*

*Under the Flood,
Deep in the mud,
Q is for Quiet...*

*The world is judged...
 ...changed.*

R is for Rainbow.

After the Flood
God said,

"I have set my rainbow in the clouds,
and it will be the sign of the covenant
between me and the earth...

Never again will the waters
become a flood to destroy all life.
Whenever the rainbow appears in the clouds,
I will see it and remember
the everlasting covenant..."

Genesis 8:22 - 9:16 NIV

S is for Singing!

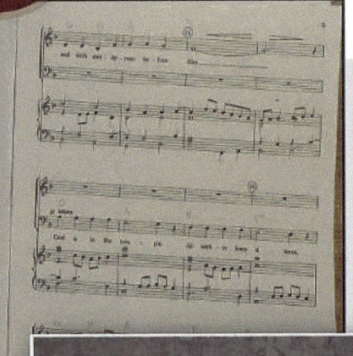

"Sing and make *music* from your heart to the Lord!" Ephesians 5:19 NIV

"The LORD answered Job... when I laid the earth's foundation ...all the stars sang together..." Job 38:1-7 NIV

T is for Truth.

Prince Rilian stolen!
Lied to and tricked!
Afraid of the sun, of his dad...
All was mixed.
The green lady seemed to be good...
What a witch!
Jack Jack was (almost!)
In the same fix...!

Daily it happens
In much the same way;
Kids are taught bad's good,
And good starts to sway.
God gave a book
That shows who is right;
That book is the Bible,
God's word, truth and light.

U is for Ultramundane.

According to Webster, 1828,
the gist of this word
is "out of this world".
Speaking of which,
A far-distant planet
With red rings
*   and blue rings,*
Rotates and twirls...

U *is for Uranus!*

V is for Venus.

*Neighbor planet of Earth,
Sometimes it's called
The evening star.*

W is for Worship.

God designed us to run and to dance, to love and exult, worshiping Him. Like a race car that's made to burn gas (and go fast!) we are designed for worshiping Him! A race car with ice cream inside of its gas tank would chug to a stop not able to go. Just so, we get messed up when we worship idols and don't worship God, our Creator and Lord.

X is for eXit...
a place to go out.

Jesus said, "I am the door. If anyone enters by Me, he will be saved and will come in and go out and find pasture."
John 10:9 HCSB

We are the sheep
Of the Good Shepherd,
Jesus.
He watches;
He keeps us
Safe in His care.

Y is for Yoke.

It links strength to strength that work may be done.

We're tired;
We're working;
We're pulling and sweating.
Jesus calls, "Take up MY yoke, my son."
His strength lifts our burden;
He's gentle and soothing.
To rest He's inviting,
"Don't worry, Dear One".

Thank you, Roger (and Barney and Allie) for your patience with me while I have worked on this little book. I thank God too for His faithful provision; His love and His Word sustain us. "His mercy endures forever." Psalm 136 NKJV

Dana E. McKee was manager and photographer for PBR Studios for many years. She is a homemaker, Bible student, editor, teacher, hair-cutter, and writer. Dana has been married to Roger for over thirty years, has six children, and lives in Pennsylvania.

To contact Dana, email her: aisfor_ape@yahoo.com. She welcomes your questions or comments.

CREDITS:

Cover and Page A – Ape photograph purchased from istock; small ape (orangutan) shot by daughter Ginger

Page D and K picture daughter Allie. Page K includes Max, the cat.

Page F features nephew Joe and niece Rebecca playing Adam and Eve.

Page G is an adaptation of Ian, Josh, and Barry from Josh's wedding portraits, taken by PBR Studios. Used by permission

Page H is brother Paul playing Jesus.

Page I shows part of former daughter-in-law Robin's face.

Pages J, W, and X include photos Dana took at Colonial Williamsburg's Historic Area during Roger and Dana's 30th anniversary trip. The pictures are used with permission of the Colonial Williamsburg Foundation. (Page J is a modified shot of a balladeer, singing and playing at Colonial Williamsburg, the evening of 03-22-2010.)

Page L shows husband Roger working hard building our deck; Page P is Roger's hands.

Page M – Monarch butterfly shot by son Barnabas.

Pages N and Q picture fossil of small invertebrates given to Dana by Denise Villani. Denise's mom found it.

The O page features a box of WalMart brand oats, modified label.

Page S shows friends and family celebrating with us our 25th wedding anniversary at our Sovereign Grace church in Joppa, MD, (then called Chesapeake Community Church.) Star shot is Spiral Galaxy M74, image credit NASA, ESA, and The Hubble Heritage.

Page T – Prince Rilian is a character from C. S. Lewis' book *The Silver Chair*; Jack Jack refers to the baby in Brad Bird's "The Incredibles," a Pixar production.

Page U's picture of Uranus is credited to the University of Wisconsin-Madison Space Science and Engineering Center, and Lawrence Sromovsky. (Psalm 19:1, NIV – "The heavens declare the glory of God.")

Page W includes a huge worship service at a Sovereign Grace church in Gaithersburg, MD (top), Bruton Parish Episcopal Church in Williamsburg, VA (middle), and a baptism service at Liberty Christian Fellowship in Seven Valleys, PA, (bottom). Pictured are Pastor Bob, Novella, Dave (being baptized), and Pastor Bill.

Page X cites verses from the Gospel of John. "Going out/coming in" indicates times of peace. In Numbers 27:17 the phrase illustrates guidance as Joshua is being commissioned to take Israel into the Promised Land; in Deuteronomy 31:2-Moses also speaks of going out/coming in. There this seems to speak of strength and authority in a realm.

Page Y shows a yoke from the Tuolumne County Museum in Sonora, CA, as well as son Ben.

Page Z – grandson Oren is pictured, as well as McWilliams brothers Mr. Palmer Jr., and Mr. Dennis.

Working with PBR Studios' equipment/lab, Dana did photography and layout work for this book. Used by permission.